a girl's guide to
dating

a girl's guide to
dating

liz wilde

illustrations by
chris long

RYLAND
PETERS
& SMALL

LONDON NEW YORK

Designer Sonya Nathoo
Editor Miriam Hyslop
Production Manager Patricia Harrington
Art Director Gabriella Le Grazie
Publishing Director Alison Starling

*First published in the United States
in 2005 by Ryland Peters & Small
519 Broadway
5th Floor
New York, NY 10012
www.rylandpeters.com*

*Text, design, and illustrations
© Ryland Peters & Small 2005*

10 9 8 7 6 5 4 3 2 1

Printed and bound in China

ISBN 1 84172 861 6

contents

introduction

Whether you have been single for a while or feel stuck in an unhappy relationship, *A Girl's Guide to Dating* will help you maximize your chances of meeting someone new.

Do you ever tell yourself that all the good guys are taken, or that the ones still available are single because no one else wants them? Or do you believe that the right "one" will come along eventually if you wait around long enough?

These are great excuses for not making an effort to put yourself out there or for staying in a bad relationship. Be honest. In order for you to meet someone new, would they have to throw themselves over the hood of your car or pull a chair up in front of your TV? Have you considered that there might be guys out there saying (or at least thinking) the same thing, and including you in that group of leftovers?

We all want the same thing: someone to love us for who we are. There are 82 million singles in the United States—there must be a few good bets among them. And with over 1,170,000 divorces every year in the U.S., even if you feel you've missed out the first time around, there are plenty of people out there looking for a new partner. Waiting for fate to throw you a soul mate is like waiting for your next employer to recognize your potential and tap you on the shoulder in your local coffee shop. If your favorite classic film is *An Officer and a Gentleman* and you secretly believe that one day your prince will come (hopefully resembling a young Richard Gere), you need to wise up.

The definition of crazy is doing the same thing over and over again and expecting a different outcome. If your efforts to meet the right man have so far come to nothing, it's time to change direction. If you want anything in life, whether it's a good job or a good man, you have to go after it. It's not at all desperate, just pro-active. The romance comes *after* you've found a great guy, not in the search process.

So forget the myths and concentrate on the facts. The way to maximize your chances of meeting someone new is to be where you will meet him, and be the sort of person you want to attract. This book tells you how...

getting
started

Decide today to stop making
excuses and start taking positive
steps towards meeting the man
of your dreams. It's your choice—
no one can do it for you.

date different men

Banish any thought that dating lots of men is somehow shameful. Meeting plenty of guys is a good thing for many reasons. Expecting to find your soul mate on your first (or second) date is not only setting yourself up for major disappointment, but also ignoring all the fun you could be having while you're searching for him. Here are a few good reasons to start dating.

Discover who you're attracted to

If you're constantly going for guys that remind you of your past (failed) relationships, take dating different men as an opportunity to do a little soul searching. You may love men who are passionate about their work, but remember how it used to drive you crazy when your ex phoned the office every five minutes while you were on vacation? Dating lots of guys lets you discover patterns in your attraction and whether they're working for or against you. What if you try dating the opposite of who you've been attracted to for a while, just to see what you've been missing?

You're not alone

When you start dating regularly you'll see how many other singles are out there wanting a relationship—and how great it feels to be attractive to the opposite sex! There's nothing like being desired to put a spring in your step.

Practice makes perfect

If you don't use it, you'll lose it. As with everything, the more you date, the better you will get at it. Dating lots of men will help you learn how to behave on a date and, most importantly, how to feel comfortable with someone new. Many of us go to pieces when sitting opposite someone we're attracted to, but practice makes perfect—and what a fun skill to learn!

Meet new people

When you date, you get to do nice things you may not otherwise find time for in your busy life. You go to restaurants, watch films, listen to bands, and generally (hopefully) get treated better than you would if you were out with a friend. And even if this man's not the one for you, he may make a good friend in the future. If you approach dating as a way to meet new people and form new relationships, rather than "the" relationship, you'll take the pressure off and enjoy the experience so much more. Look upon dating as a way to expand your social life and experience new things. Who knows? You may discover a new passion (modern art/Japanese food) at the same time as a great new man.

It's better to have loved and lost, than never to have loved at all.

Lord, Alfred Tennyson

your dating mindset

All the dates in the world won't find you the right guy if you don't have the right attitude.

Give the guy a chance
Many of us think that if it's true love, we'll know the instant we meet someone. But that's not love, that's sexual chemistry. There are many factors that contribute to a great relationship and it's impossible to evaluate them all in the first five minutes. So relax, ignore his Velcro-fastening sneakers and get to know the guy. You can always take him shoe shopping on your third date.

Lust is not always love
And, talking of sexual chemistry, that amphetamine-like high is not necessarily love but nature's way of bonding you during the early stages of a relationship. So enjoy the hormone rush but don't make any rash decisions (mortgage, marriage, meeting his mother) until your body has calmed down a little.

You have more than one soul mate
If you've just come out of a relationship, it's tempting to think you've already met your one true love. Not true. The world's population is well over six billion, so believing there's only one mate for you among all that lot is ignoring a considerable number of possibilities.

Your past doesn't have to be your future

So you've had failed relationships? So has every other single person. What's important is to learn from your mistakes so you don't repeat them. If you constantly go for losers, look at your self-esteem. You can't expect anyone else to treat you well if you always come last on your own list of priorities. Write down a list of all your strengths, and read it every day. Finish something you've always wanted to (a degree, a marathon, a relationship), and face a big fear—it's the biggest self-esteem booster of all!

Don't waste time on lost causes

Whether you're hankering after an ex-boyfriend, or someone who's not available/not interested, no new date will ever match up to the fantasy in your head of how wonderful your life could be if you were with him. Remember: if he doesn't want to be with you, then he's hardly your perfect man, and who wants a relationship in their head when they can have a living, breathing one? You need to make the decision to get out there. How much longer are you going to put your life on hold for this guy?

Stop searching for Mr. Perfect

There's no such thing as the perfect person (are *you*?), so if that's who you're holding out for, you'll be in for a long wait. Instead, decide on the things that are important to you (humor, kindness, fresh breath) and be willing to compromise. This isn't about lowering your standards; it's just accepting that even Brad Pitt would reveal the odd annoying habit once you got to know him.

Be the sort of person you want to attract

We attract people and situations according to how we're thinking and feeling, so if you truly believe there are no good men out there, you're more likely to attract guys who reinforce that belief. Instead, work on improving your outlook on life. No one wants to date a moaner, and guess what? If you spend your time complaining about your job, friends, and family, you'll automatically attract a partner who thinks exactly the same way. Not exactly a barrel of laughs. And what's the rush? If you can hear your biological clock ticking, then chances are he can as well!

Don't see every man as marriage material

The best way to enjoy dating is to look at it as a chance to widen your social life, rather than regarding every man as your potential partner. If you see dating as an opportunity to spend a nice evening out talking to someone new, then you're far more likely to relax and enjoy yourself. Remember: the way to win is to make it OK to lose.

confidence tricks

The amount of confidence you feel in any situation is in line with to the story you're telling yourself about your past success. If you approach dating with a negative story playing continuously in your head ("I'm so bad at this, he's going to be bored, I wish I was more interesting"), you are more likely to have a negative experience.

The more you think you're a dud date, the more he's likely to agree with you. But confidence can be faked. You can actually trick your mind into feeling more confident in a situation by focusing on what else may be possible, even if your past experiences don't back you up.

For example, a boxer would never walk into a ring expecting to be knocked down in the first round, so don't walk into a bar expecting your date to be disappointed. Your level of confidence enhances your performance in every area of life, whether sporting or personal victory.

Fact: if you act confident, men will treat you as if you are. And confidence breeds confidence, leading you to act in a way you would have previously never thought possible.

On the inside

* See yourself in your mind as how you want to be. Think back to when you last felt confident (a success, a compliment, a great night out), and take that feeling to your date.

* Concentrate on staying physically relaxed. Tension mixed with confidence can come over as arrogant and cocky. That's not confident—just annoying.

* Fake it until you make it, and act as if you're confident. How would you stand? What would you say? How would your voice sound? What expression would be on your face?

* What makes you feel upbeat and confident? Dancing around your bedroom to a specific song? Going on an endorphin-fueled run? Chatting with your funniest friend? Then do it before your date. Do whatever it takes to lift your spirits and send you off on your date with a positive frame of mind.

* Put together a two-minute show-reel in your mind of your most confident moments (a bit like the football highlights you see on TV) and then press the replay button every time you need a moral-boosting reminder.

On the outside

* The secret of dressing to impress is to make sure you're the one who's impressed. Everyone has their own taste in clothes so you're best dressing to suit yourself rather than second-guessing what your date may like. So some men like high heels, but if they make you walk like a duck then stick to your usual flats. We all have a favorite outfit in the closet, and if you're wearing something that makes you feel good, you're naturally going to look great, too.

* Remember: unless it's a blind date, he asked you out because he likes what you look like. So don't even think of changing to please him—he's keen already. Oh, and if he comments on how great you look, what he actually means is he really, really fancies you...

x Wear your best underwear even if you've got no intention of letting him see it. Sexy undies will give you far more confidence than those gray panties with the frayed elastic.

* Go for the no-visible-make-up look, even if it's taken you hours to achieve. No man likes a woman to look like she's plastered with make-up, and they're not overly impressed with hairstyling products either. A little something to give your hair oomph is fine, but make sure your hair still moves like nature intended it to.

* Smell is our most powerful sense and the one most associated with memory, so leave a lasting impression by wearing a light, fresh fragrance. Hair holds scent longer than skin, so spray a little on your hairbrush before your final style.

* There are more subtle ways of showing you're interested than dribbling out of the corner of your mouth. Body language experts advise leaning in towards him slightly and also pointing your knees and feet in his direction. Don't cross your arms as you'll look ultra-defensive, and don't fiddle with your body—pulling on your ear, covering your mouth, or picking your nails all show a lack of confidence and can also be pretty annoying to watch. Crazy about him? Then hold his gaze for at least three seconds, as this is the biggest giveaway that you're impressed with what you see.

* If all this sounds too contrived, practice the type of look you'd give someone you like if you met up by chance at a party. Then use the same big, friendly smile and open body language on any man you'd like to know better.

where to *meet*

Dating can seem so scary, it might be tempting to stay at home instead. After all, there's always something on TV. But that won't help you meet the man of your dreams.

the traditional way

First, you need to believe there are many men out there who would love to date someone like you. Second, you have to maximize your chances of meeting as many of them as possible. The more men you meet, the more likelihood there is that one of them is going to be perfect for you.

Ask your friends

This age-old method is responsible for many happy couples. Not surprising really, as your friends know you well enough to have a good idea of the kind of guy you'll get on with. And blind dates don't have to be blind. Ask to see a photo first, so you know who you're letting yourself in for.

Accept invitations

It's a numbers game. The more people you meet, the more likely you'll find someone fabulous. And don't make the mistake of only talking to men. That woman you met at the bar may become the friend that sets you up with her gorgeous brother. Weddings are traditionally a great place to meet a man, but adopt a certain nonchalance in catching the bouquet to ensure you don't appear as the "When will it be my turn?" type of girl. Other people's office parties are also great for meeting men as you won't have the potential embarrassment of having to share a photocopier, should things go sour.

Join a club/take up a new activity

Do you love running? Always fancied cycling? If you join a club to do something you're interested in, you'll find men there with the same interests as you. A very good place to start. And gym memberships are so expensive you'll have to go at least twice a week to justify the cost, so you're guaranteed to bump into any guys you fancy on a regular basis. Even better, take up a new sport or activity that requires a partner. Check to see if your local tennis or squash club will pair you up with other singles. Or try salsa dancing and get to dance with a whole roomful of men every night!

Sign up for an evening class

OK, this is a cliché, but you'll get to learn something new and, if you meet a guy, you'll have something in common to talk about. Choose photography or French rather than flower arranging or needlepoint, for obvious reasons.

Volunteer yourself

If your ideal man is kind and caring, chances are you'll find his type by volunteering yourself for a worthwhile cause. Just make sure you choose something you're passionate about or he'll see through you right away! Plus research has shown that helping others is guaranteed to boost your own self-esteem.

If you see a man you like

When meeting someone new, research says it takes at least three contacts to determine mutual interest before it's OK to take it further. So, say you fancy someone at the gym...

* The purpose of your first contact is to leave him with a good impression of you. Make eye contact and smile. Perhaps take a trip to the water cooler at the same time as he does, and make small talk. You could pay him a compliment (if you really mean it) or just be friendly.

* The second contact is designed to find out a little more about him and note a positive or negative response. Now you've spoken once, it's easier to ask a couple of questions. How often does he get the chance to work out? Is he training for anything in particular?

* The third contact is the one where you get to check his availability. Chat a bit further about anything from last time and then say, "It's really nice talking to you—I don't suppose you'd like a juice later?"

If this seems way too scary, repeat the second contact as many times as you like until you feel more confident. You never know, he may beat you to it!

give fate a helping hand

The U.S. dating services industry is a $1.08 billion business. It may seem strange interacting with strangers, but it sure beats sitting in a bar waiting for the perfect partner to fall into your lap.

Internet dating

Get over the idea that internet daters are all geeks. Online dating is pro-active, not pathetic. You're both there for the same reason so there's none of that "I wonder if he wants a relationship" angst, and you're likely to meet men you wouldn't meet in your everyday life (lawyer, doctor, tree surgeon). Also, the databases of most sites are so huge you're almost guaranteed to get lots of replies once you've posted your details. If nothing else, it's a great ego boost!

Take the time to be very specific when writing your profile (the type of relationship you want, what's important to you, etc). You may get fewer responses, but the ones you do get will be worth following up. Have a nice photo taken, as profiles with photos get far more responses. One of the most popular hits is www.Udate.com, which has two million members worldwide.

Speed dating

This is all about meeting as many men as possible in one evening.
An equal number of men and women attend each event. Couples
sit at tables around the room. The host then rings a bell after a short
time (five to ten minutes) and the men will move on to the next table.
The organizer then lets you know if there was a mutual interest during
the evening and gives contact information to you both in case you
want to take it further.

Speed dating is perfect if you're not sure about going on one-to-one
dates and love the idea of meeting lots of potential partners in
a couple of hours (and can cope with what may seem like 20 job
interviews!). But if the idea of having to sum up another person in
a matter of minutes (or, worse still, being summed up) is your idea of
hell, then don't do it. To see if there are local events in your area, check
out www.8minutedating.com.

Classified ads

Advertising yourself is quick, cheap, and easy, and most local
newspapers, not to mention nationals and listings magazines,
have sections at the back traditionally called "lonely hearts." Most
of these publications will act as the middleman and collect your
replies before passing them on to you. The main problem is that

you don't get to see a picture as you do with Internet dating, but the personals are updating their image with Talking Ads. Look for ads with a phone number you can ring to leave a message—if the man's interested, he'll call you back.

Vacations for singles

There are many travel companies with vacation packages designed specifically for singles—ask at your local travel agent. A special interest vacation (hiking up the Himalayas, a yoga retreat) will also ensure you meet like-minded people.

Dating agencies

Personal introduction agencies can be pretty pricey, but they do a lot of the legwork for you, and because of the cost, you're likely to get a more exclusive type of clientele. Choose an agency that conducts personal interviews rather than sending out a postal questionnaire, and before you hand over your money, ask the size of their client base and how long they continue to search on your behalf. Don't be shy about asking for exactly what you want. Men tend to exaggerate their positive attributes more than women, so if you don't set your standards high, you may get the geek still living with his mother. For safety, check that the agency won't give out your surname, address, or home phone number without your permission.

Safety tips

* Choose a dating agency that asks for proof of I.D. and an Internet site with a "double-blind" messaging system which means emails are directed through the site rather than straight to your own inbox. And make sure your agency is a member of a professional association.

* Insist on a couple of email-only weeks to reveal any potential psychotic tendencies. For extra safety, set up a new email account so you can ditch the account if you want to ditch him.

* Make sure you speak on the phone at least once before meeting— you can tell a lot about a person by their voice. And don't be afraid to ask lots of questions, as this is your chance to find out how many hours he spends watching football...

* Don't give out information about your home address or place of work on the first date, and don't accept a lift or go back to your date's house until you're absolutely sure you can trust him.

* Meet in a public place, give your date's name and telephone number to a friend, and take your cell phone to call them when you're on your way home. For more safety info visit: www.personalsafetyonline.com.

Escape strategies

* Arrange for a friend to be already positioned at the meeting place so you have a reassuring backup should things go wrong. A nod in their direction followed by "Oh, how great to see you—come and join us!" could save a potentially tortuous evening.

* Ask a friend to call you an hour into your date. If you're bored senseless (or worse), you can get off the phone claiming an emergency. "My friend's forgotten her key and I'm the only one with a spare one" will get you out the door.

* For a daytime date, borrow a dog and say you need to get it back to its owner in an hour. It's a great ice-breaker, too.

* Don't feel you have to stay all night if there's absolutely no chemistry between you. There's no shame in being honest, but be gentle. "I'm not sure we're made for each other but it's been really nice meeting you" will free you after an hour without having to dodge his calls for weeks afterwards.

* Don't take it personally if you meet a few no-hopers along the way. This date may have been a dead loss but the next one may be the best date of your life!

first date

A great first date depends on two things: being a great date and enjoying yourself. And you may be surprised to learn that both of these are in your control. So here's how to ensure you have a great first date.

be a great date

*If you think your dating technique is a little rusty, don't panic. Being
great company has more to do with your decision to make the effort
than some skill you were never taught at school. So relax and simply
be who you want to attract—a guaranteed way to ensure he likes
you, if you like him!*

Be on time

Research the location as you would before a job interview, so you
know how to get there and the time it will take. Being punctual shows
you're not flaky and, most importantly, that you consider your date's
time valuable (i.e., he has better things to do than hang around
waiting for you to show up!).

Be prepared

Talking of job interviews, you could do worse than approach your
date as if you're preparing to impress a potential employer. What do
you know about your interviewer? What do you want your interviewer
to know about you? How can you work this into your conversation?

Be yourself

It's one thing to present yourself in your best light, quite another to
reinvent yourself into something you're not. Lying about culinary skills
that would give Jamie Oliver sleepless nights or a "glamorous"

job that's actually more table-setting than jet-setting will only leave you red-faced later. Have the confidence to be who you are and if the date goes well, you'll know he likes you—and not the promise of a Michelin star meal.

Don't tell him too much

The first date is not the time to share details of your last break-up, food allergies, or childhood shoplifting conviction. You're out for a good time, not a free therapy session, so avoid serious topics until you know him better. A little mystery is a good thing, so leave him wanting more—not feeling he knows you better than his own mother!

Let him get a word in

When we're nervous we have a habit of jumping in quickly to fill any (shock, horror) silences. But frenzied conversation is exhausting for you and boring for him. Remember, you came out with this person to learn more about him, so allow him to tell you. You'll get far more information if you pay attention to him rather than trying to impress with your stand-up comedy routine.

Be approachable

Wear something you feel comfortable in that's not a million miles away from what you were wearing when you first met (if you have already).

Make eye contact when you talk—avoiding his gaze just makes you look insecure (or shifty!), and watch your body language. Relaxed is good, crossed arms and legs (and fingers) is not. He'll feel like he's interrogating you, not dating you.

Have an opinion
First dates are full of anxious moments, so help him out by telling him what you want. "Oh, I don't mind" is not only annoying, it's probably a lie, too. So when he asks if you want to get something to eat, tell the truth. And if you know somewhere nice, recommend that too. He'll be grateful not to have all the responsibility himself.

Be polite
Say thank you and be kind. You may even want to offer to pay (even if you're hoping he'll refuse). Remember, what goes around comes around...

Don't let him do all the work
Go out with the intention of having a good time— even if you end up having to amuse yourself! Taking responsibility for your own happiness is far more attractive than simply sitting back and expecting him to entertain you.

enjoy the date

How to turn any date into a pleasurable experience—no matter who you're with!

Keep things in perspective

This is a date, not a life-threatening experience. If things don't go well, does it really matter? It's just a date and will end, so try to make the most of it. Find something to enjoy—the food, the film, or even the scenery—and, if nothing else, this will help you decide who you don't want to go out with so you can choose a little more wisely next time.

Do something you love

A foolproof way to enjoy any date is to plan an activity you love— no matter who you're with. And focusing on doing something more interesting than sipping a glass of wine will also give you less time to worry about what impression you're making. Suggest anything you enjoy—an art exhibition, a band, a comedy club—and you'll also have something to talk about on your second date.

Keep it short

If you're not sure you have anything in common, arrange a date with a time limit. Knowing you can only spend an hour with him will make the date much less scary. Lunchtime, when you both have to get back to work, is perfect. An evening when you have an early start the next day is another way to keep it short, but warn him beforehand or he might think you're making a run for it! And if it's a blind date, a mid-morning coffee ensures a quick and easy exit. Keep the first-date brief and you'll leave him wishing for more, not wondering how to escape.

Avoid unrealistic expectations

If you secretly hope this guy will be the one, you're not only putting massive pressure on one meeting, you're also setting yourself up for a big disappointment if things don't work out. So rather than expecting to be swept off your feet, intend to have a great time whatever. That way you can relax and enjoy being out with someone new. And if it's terrible, you won't be crushed—and you need never see him again!

Be positive

Approach your date with a positive frame of mind, what we focus on is what we see, so if you've convinced yourself he'll be bored with your conversation, you'll be looking for evidence every time his eyes wander for a second. No one stands a chance against those odds.

Concentrate on him

Instead of worrying about what he thinks of you, concentrate on what you think about him. Most of us are starved of attention and love nothing more than to be listened to, so do him the favor of really listening. Ask questions and be interested in the answers. He'll come away thinking you're the most interesting person on the planet! And if you're concerned about topics of conversation, be sure to read a newspaper that day so you can chat about current events.

Be present
Stay in the present rather than obsessing about the past or future. Resist the urge to compare him to your ex-boyfriend ("Oh no, Adam did that and turned into a complete control freak!"), or sit there wondering if this could be the man you're going to marry and have six children with. All your past relationships are over and you can never know what the future holds.

Have fun
If you don't like Chinese food, don't sit there all night picking at your stir-fry noodles. Instead, suggest an alternative – even if he's pre-booked. How's he to know what you like unless you tell him? Someone who's having a good time is far more attractive than someone worrying about their MSG allergy.

Gravitation can not be held responsible for people falling in love.

Albert Einstein

and finally... the goodbye

A bad ending can ruin the best of dates, so be prepared. Ask yourself near the end of the date, "Where do I want things to go from here?" and take the action needed to make this happen. Chances are he'll be more tongue-tied than you, so take control.

The end of the date can be an awkward moment for both of you, so if he's standing around looking at his feet, help him out by asking for what you want. If you want him to kiss you, say, "Would you like to kiss me goodnight?" If you want to see him again, say, "Would you like to go out next week?" How can he know you're interested if you don't show it? The sad truth is, there would be far more second dates if both parties weren't left wondering what the other one wanted.

How far to take things? Do what feels right for you, not what you "should do" (no tongues on the first date), or what you feel obliged to do (well, that meal was expensive...). Do what you want and you'll not only enjoy the experience, you'll also have no regrets.

If you don't think you're a match made in heaven, be prepared to let him down gently. "Actually, I'm really busy for the next three weeks" may be the coward's way out, but it still works if you can't bring yourself to tell the truth about his halitosis. Just because he's not marriage material doesn't mean he has no place in your life.

second date
(and beyond)

You've both decided there's
enough attraction to meet again
and, with no first date nerves to
worry about, this really is where
the fun can start.

are we in love yet?

On your second date, you should feel a little more relaxed and can start to find out more about him and what you have in common.

But don't get so relaxed that you start telling him about how you stalked your ex-boyfriend or the design of your dream wedding dress. It's also too soon to take him to a family event or introduce him as your boyfriend should you bump into a friend.

We all love labels, as it helps us make sense of what's going on around us. So chances are, by your fifth date you'll be wanting to call him your boyfriend. You can be pretty sure he feels the same way if his family and friends seem to know about you, and when you call him at work the person taking the message knows who you are.

Just because you're madly in love, don't ignore the warning bells. If he told you on your first date he was planning to move back to England next year, don't spend the next 12 months hoping he'll change his mind. Chances are you'll be the one sobbing into your hankie at the airport. And watch out for signs that he's far from serious—such as not returning your calls, only seeing you on a week night or keeping you away from his friends. The first few months of a relationship are supposed to be the most passionate, so if he's treating you as a low priority now, things will only get worse.

is he your soul mate?

The perfect man doesn't exist. Just as you have the odd flaw (go on, admit it), deluding yourself that anyone else is perfect is setting yourself up for major disappointment. Contrary to popular myth, love is not blind. Parents love their children despite their faults. What is short-sighted is infatuation, and that's what you're feeling if all you can see is perfection. But ignore the rest at your peril. Everyone has faults and, if you haven't seen his yet, you better get ready as he won't be able to hide them for long!

Your soul mate is really your goal mate. Someone who shares the same priorities in life as you. Who thinks the same about the things that really matter. Not that he needs to be a mirror image of you. It's just important to agree on your non-negotiable requirements (marriage, children, values) to ensure you're heading in roughly the same direction. So if his taste in music gives you a headache, it doesn't mean the relationship's doomed. You just need to buy him some good-quality headphones.

Love is such a big word, it really should have more letters.

Kobi Yamada

The Soul Mate Test

To discover whether or not you've met your "right one", answer the following questions:

* Do you admire and respect him enough to actually want to be a little more like him? What can he teach you that you know would be good for you to learn? And I don't just mean car maintenance. Do you admire his patience? His loyalty to friends and family? His ability to stick to a decision no matter who tries to change his mind?

* If his personality stays exactly the same as it is now (for another year or ten), would he still make you happy? So you might want him to be a bit more affectionate, or a more attentive listener. But if all your nagging doesn't change him (and it won't), would you still be happy with exactly who he is today?

* When you think of him, do you get a warm, fuzzy feeling inside? Does he make you feel good about yourself? Does he encourage you to improve your quality of life? His untidiness, snoring, and passion for football may drive you mad, but it's the big things that really matter.

be a great girlfriend

Be a great girlfriend and he'll be putty in your hands. Here's how:

* Tell the truth. If you had a great time, tell him. If you didn't, tell him what would improve it next time. Treat him like your best friend (he's on your side!) and, if he makes you feel good, tell him.

* If you want to find out how angry or dissatisfied you are, just put a man in your life. If you dislike yourself or the world, chances are you'll take it out on him before long. The truth is, constantly criticizing your partner probably means it's you you're unhappy with. Not many men get to go out with someone who's happy with their life—be that person and you'll be very attractive.

* Don't give up everything for him. You want him to fit into your great life, not the other way around, so keep doing all the things you enjoyed before you met him. Otherwise he might turn around in six months and wonder where the lively, interesting person he fell in love with has disappeared to.

* The same goes for suspicion. Not an attractive trait. What would happen if you always assumed he was acting from the best possible motivation unless proven wrong? How much more fun would your relationship be?

great expectations

*The most common cause of relationship frustration (and failure)
is unrealistic expectations. Relationships may look perfect in the
movies, but even film stars go home to partners that slob out in front
of the TV and occasionally forget their birthday. Remember, this is a
real relationship, not a celluloid fantasy, and your partner is a human
being, not a character in a film created to fulfill women's fantasies.
You're no Stepford wife (hopefully), so don't expect your man to be
a cardboard-cut-out hero either.*

If he loved me he'd know what I was thinking

You might think all-day sulking makes it obvious that you're angry
that he forgot your birthday, but he's probably more likely to dismiss it
as a bad day, or P.M.T. Expecting your partner to be a mind-reader is
setting yourself up for constant frustration, so if he's upset you tell him
the reason. The real one.

If he loved me we'd never argue

Fights are inevitable, but make sure the topic is really worth it before
you let rip. Remember: you're supposed to love him! Keep it
brief (once you've made your point, drop it), and if you're in the
wrong, admit it. No one's perfect (remember?) and he'll be
far more likely to do the same when he's in the wrong
next time.

If he loved me he'd change to make me happy

Do you have a long list of requirements that no one can ever quite live up to? If you keep searching for this perfect man, who only exists in your head, you're going to pass up some great human beings. It's very common to go through partners repeating the same old mistakes, and strangely we naturally seem to choose men who push our buttons. So if the same issues come up time and again, chances are it's you and your fantasy that need to change, not him.

If he loved me he'd do what I asked

Not true, and would you really want a mindless boyfriend? If you get angry or upset every time he says no, chances are you'll either get a yes that never comes true or an argument. Neither of which will get you what you want. The trick is to ask in a way that includes some benefit for him, and learn to accept a no (even if it's through gritted teeth) that will make a yes next time far more likely.

If he loved me he'd understand me

Women are a mystery to most men. They will rarely guess what you mean beyond the actual words you're saying so you either need to state your case directly, or leave your deeper contemplations for those Chardonnay nights with your girlfriends.

if things
go wrong

Breaking up is never easy to do, but it's
better (and braver) to make the decision
than prolong the hurt. Of course, parting
is never nice at the time, but it's actually far
less painful than living in a constant state
of disappointment.

if he stops calling

*You've had a great two months (or so you thought), and then,
suddenly, he goes quiet on you. It's never easy to admit you're wrong
about something (or someone), but the reality is that, if he doesn't
feel the same way about you, he's not a man who can make you happy.*

Just because he's decided he doesn't want a relationship doesn't mean
you're fat/ugly/have terrible table manners. It could mean many things,
and most of them have nothing to do with you. He may just not want
to be committed right now. He may have a preconceived idea of his
perfect partner and something about you doesn't fit (his loss…). Or he
may just have got back with the ex he's secretly been in love with for
the last six months. None of which make him your perfect partner, so
spending more time on him would just be a waste.

If you're convinced there's something worth saving, leave it a week
before ringing and stay calm. Don't demand to know where he's been;
just ask if he fancies a night out. If he's off-hand or doesn't return your
message, you know you've given it your best shot. No desperate,
needy letter, text, or email, please. The only four letters you should be
concerned with are N-E-X-T. The most important thing to remember in
any break-up is not to take it personally. It's vital you separate yourself
from the situation...

if you're just settling

Do you have more bad moments than good? Does he make you more stressed than happy? Be honest. Are you really only still with him because you're scared no one else will put up with your snoring?

So many relationships continue way past their normal expiration because no one makes a decision. Things aren't too bad, after all. But no decision, is a decision. If you were aboard a sinking ship, not choosing to hop on a lifeboat is the same as choosing to go down with the wreck. The simple fact is this: spending more time on the wrong person is time you could be spending with the right one. But before you throw in the towel, take one more look at the relationship. What could you do to make it better? There's no point moaning that he never takes you out any more when you spend most evenings glued to *Sex and the City* DVDs with your friends. What are you blaming on him that you could take responsibility for?

Are you low on his list of priorities simply because he knows he's low on yours? Do you constantly criticize him and then wonder why he prefers watching football with his pals? Remember: be the kind of person you want to be with. Put yourself in his shoes. Would you be happy going out with you? Do you make him feel good about himself? Do you bring out the best in him, or the worst?

if he breaks your heart

You can't be sure anyone will be in your life forever, but you can be sure you'll be with yourself for the rest of your life. So become someone you enjoy spending time with.

You probably made some changes during your relationship, so now's the time to decide if you want to stick with them or not. Celebrate the fact that you can choose exactly what you want to do, when you want to do it (a luxury most people can only dream of).

Spend more time with friends, especially the ones you didn't have time for while you were seeing him. Make a list of the people you haven't called for a while, and don't worry if they haven't called you either. It doesn't mean they don't like you any more; they've just been busy—like you. And increase the amount of pleasure in your life by showing yourself affection. Arrange your surroundings so they give you a boost and do at least one pleasurable thing for yourself every single day.

Three grand essentials to happiness
in this life are something to do,
something to love,
and something to hope for.

Joseph Addison

happy endings

"I met my boyfriend at a wedding. We were both in a bit of a soppy mood and thinking 'Ahh!' as the couple looked so happy. Weddings are a great excuse to really dress up and look your best, plus the all-day drinking helps! My boyfriend just sat down next to me, something he says he would never have done if we'd been out at a club."

"My husband and I met on an internet dating site. We emailed each other for a couple of weeks, so by the time he plucked up the courage to pick up the phone I felt I knew him already. But it wasn't until he took so much trouble booking the restaurant for our first date that I realized I was smitten."

"I always find gyms a great place to meet men. The down side is you have to exercise like you mean it, as fit men are definitely attracted to fit women. I've met my last three boyfriends at a gym, but I won't be meeting any more as I've just got engaged!"

"I split up with my boyfriend and felt really low, so a friend suggested going on a date. It was the best thing I could have done. I got so much attention from the men around the table that I left with my confidence fully restored; plus, of the three who contacted me afterwards, one is now my husband."

"My roommate and I were both single so decided to go to a speed-dating event. We had a ball, but speaking to all those different men made me realize that my roommate was actually the one for me. It just goes to show you sometimes don't notice who's right under your nose!"

"I met my boyfriend on a 'cruise dating' night. We each had a list of eight 30-minute dates picked by the organizers according to what we were looking for in a partner. The event was held in different pubs and the men would walk between them to their next date (we had a prop on the table so they would recognize us—mine was a Kit-Kat!). At the end of the night, we all met up at one pub for a party and my boyfriend came straight over."

"A friend told me about an Internet site for people from abroad working in this country and looking for accommodation and relationships. It feels more intimate than a large dating internet site and I've been on ten dates so far. I'm now seeing two guys and they're both lovely—I guess I'm going to have to make up my mind soon!"

acknowledgments

The author would like to thank the following:

*All my wonderful friends and family; Coach U for teaching
me a better way; and Alison Starling of Ryland Peters & Small.*

*Visit Liz Wilde's website at www.wildelifecoaching.com for
information about her one-to-one coaching and online programs.
Her books* Unlock Your Potential, *and* Home Spa: Destress *, are
also published by Ryland Peters & Small.*